GREAT BRITONS

MUSICIANS

Michael Johnstone

FRANKLIN WATTS
LONDON•SYDNEY

*First published in 2007 by
Franklin Watts*

*Copyright © Franklin
Watts 2007*

*Franklin Watts
338 Euston Road
London NW1 3BH*

*Franklin Watts Australia
Level 17/207 Kent Street
Sydney, NSW 2000*

*A CIP catalogue record for
this book is available from
the British Library.*

Dewey number: 780.92

ISBN: 978 0 7496 7473 1

Printed in China

*Franklin Watts is a division
of Hachette Children's
Books, an Hachette Livre
UK company.*

*Designer: Thomas Keenes
Art Director: Jonathan Hair
Editor: Sarah Ridley
Editor-in-Chief:
John C. Miles
Picture Research:
Diana Morris*

*Picture credits:
Inside: Andrew Swannell,
ArenaPAL, Topfoto: 35. AP,
Topfoto: 33. ArenaPAL,
Topfoto: 15. Clive Barda,*

*21, 23, 24, 27. UPP,
Topfoto: 37, 43. UPPA,
Topfoto: 29. Cover: KPA,
HIP, Topfoto*

CONTENTS

INTRODUCTION

This book contains biographies of 21 outstanding British musicians. They are all composers, conductors or performers and have been chosen because they were either born in Britain, or became British. They have also been chosen because, from William Byrd in the 16th century through to Courtney Pine in the 21st century, each of them has made a significant contribution to the history of British music.

The book begins in the 1500s with the English composer William Byrd. However, there had been music in Britain for centuries before that time. Monks composed and sang beautiful chants during their religious services and people sang and danced to folk music with many different kinds of instruments. Kings and nobles paid musicians to entertain them in their palaces and to sing services in their chapels. But many of the biographical details of these musicians are unknown, unclear or simply too sketchy to write down in an accurate form.

By the 1700s, monarchs and nobles still commissioned musicians to write and perform, but many more ordinary people could attend performances when they were available. This trend continued throughout the 19th century, with large new concert halls and opera houses being built to hold ever-bigger audiences. By the 20th century, the newly invented gramophone and, later, the science of broadcasting through radio and television helped to spread the new musical forms of jazz and pop music to audiences of literally millions. These trends allowed groups such as The Beatles to become world-famous celebrities. But despite the huge audiences music has gained through radio, television and now via the ever-expanding Internet, live music remains popular worldwide.

This book is not a history of British music; it is about the men and women who made significant contributions to the musical life of Britain in many different ways. But the biographies are arranged chronologically so that reading through them you will not only learn about musicians' lives, but you will also see how British music changed and evolved.

You, of course, will have your own favourites, and will wonder why some of them are not in this book. A list such as this is always personal, and can always be changed with good reason. But it is true to say that each and every person in this book influenced British music in one way or another, and has left their mark for future generations to study, and admire.

WILLIAM BYRD
ENGLAND'S GREATEST RENAISSANCE COMPOSER

BORN London, 1540?
DIED London,
4 July 1623
AGE About 83 years

William Byrd was born at a time of religious turmoil in England, when people could be severely punished for their beliefs. Such were his skills and talents that he wrote music for use in Roman Catholic services, as well as for the Church of England.

Byrd was born sometime around 1540, but scholars still argue over the exact date. At this time England was in the process of changing from a Roman Catholic to a Protestant nation. People took religion and ways of worship very seriously; often it was a matter of life and death.

William Byrd's musical career began at a young age when he became a boy chorister (singer) in the Chapel Royal under Queen Mary I. Mary was a fervent Roman Catholic – in contrast to her staunchly Protestant half-brother Edward VI, whom she succeeded.

To be a chorister in the Queen's chapel was a great honour. Byrd would have met some of the best musicians of the day, who were employed in the Queen's service. One of the most famous was Byrd's teacher, Thomas Tallis (1505–1585). By the time he was a teenager, Byrd's own works had been performed in the Chapel Royal.

Mary I died in 1558 and was succeeded by her half-sister Elizabeth. Elizabeth I was staunchly Protestant, and it is thought that Byrd may have left the Chapel Royal for this reason. Roman Catholic religious services were gradually banned and those people who wished to worship as Catholics had to do so in secret. Byrd became organist and choirmaster of Lincoln Cathedral in his mid-twenties, but got a job in the Chapel Royal again in 1572. He moved back to London, where he worked as a singer, composer and organist for more than 20 years.

In this period many of Byrd's most famous compositions began to appear. He collaborated with Thomas Tallis on *Cantiones Sacrae* (sacred songs) in 1575. This was a collection of Latin motets (short compositions for use in church). Two further collections appeared in 1589

Most of William Byrd's compositions were written for religious services.

and 1591 but by this time Tallis had died so the pieces in these last two sets were all Byrd's own work. He also published 'Psalmes, Sonets and Songs' in 1588 and 'Songes of Sundrie Natures' in 1589. In addition to all this, Byrd produced a large amount of Anglican music for the Chapel Royal.

In 1593 Byrd moved from London to the village of Stondon Massey in Essex, where he lived for the rest of his life. Here he composed many settings of the Roman Catholic Mass and, in 1605-07, wrote *Gradualia*, a year-long musical cycle. He died in 1623 and was buried in Stondon.

One of the things that made William Byrd so remarkable was that his compositions alternated between the Anglican and Roman Catholic liturgies (ways of worshipping) at a time when one or the other was banned. It is fairly certain that Byrd was a Roman Catholic. That he was allowed to live and work without being imprisoned is a testament to the strength of the support he enjoyed from the monarch – and his own remarkable musical talent. 🏴󠁧󠁢󠁥󠁮󠁧󠁿

HENRY PURCELL
17TH-CENTURY COMPOSER OF OPERA AND INSTRUMENTAL MUSIC

BORN London,
10 September 1659
DIED London,
21 November 1695
AGE 36 years

Henry Purcell is the most famous English composer of the 17th century. Born into an exceptional musical family, he created works that are still performed today. His death at the early age of 36 robbed Britain of a musical genius at the height of his powers.

Henry Purcell was born in London. His father, who was also called Henry Purcell, was a singer in the Chapel Royal and sang at the coronation of King Charles II in 1661. When his father died in 1664, young Henry was looked after by his uncle, Thomas Purcell, who was also a singer in His Majesty's Chapel Royal. Thomas was kind to young Henry and arranged for the boy to become a chorister.

As a chorister at the Chapel Royal, Purcell studied music with two well-known musicians, Captain Henry Cooke and Pelham Humfrey. When Purcell was about nine, it is said that he began to write his first compositions, although his first work that can be dated is an ode for the King's birthday, written in 1670.

After Humfrey died in 1674, Purcell continued his studies with Dr John Blow (1649–1708), one of the best-known English composers of the 17th century. A talented young musician, Purcell was appointed organist at Westminster School, which he attended. He began to write songs, suites (sets) of music to go with plays in the theatre, such as *Abdelazer* (1677), and religious music to be sung in the Chapel Royal.

The origins of opera

Opera began in the late 1500s and early 1600s, when groups of wealthy Italians decided to present ancient Greek stories set to music. These entertainments took the form of arias, recitatives and choruses acted out on stage. One of the most important early operas was *Orfeo* by **CLAUDIO MONTEVERDI** (1567–1643). By the late 17th century, opera had become very popular in Europe.

In 1680 Blow, who had been organist of Westminster Abbey in London since 1669, resigned so that his young pupil could have his job. The 22-year-old Purcell stopped writing theatre music and devoted himself mainly to religious music and odes for the royal family. He married in 1682 and his first son was born that year. Purcell's first printed composition, 'Twelve Sonatas', was published the following year.

Henry Purcell is the best-known English composer of his age.

King Charles II died in 1685 and his brother James became king. Purcell wrote two of his finest sacred anthems, 'I Was Glad' and 'My Heart Is Inditing' for James II's coronation.

In 1687 Purcell began to write for the theatre again. One of his most famous works, *Dido and Aeneas*, dates from around 1688. *Dido* has been called the first English opera, in which the action is driven forward by sung passages called recitative in between arias and choruses. Purcell married his music for *Dido* to words by Nahum Tate, the Poet Laureate, to tell the story of the doomed love affair between Dido, Queen of Carthage, and Aeneas, a Trojan prince. The opera was originally written for a private performance at a girls' school in London. It is still performed regularly more than 300 years later.

The 1690s were a busy time for Purcell, as he kept up his output of operatic and religious music. Then, in 1695 Queen Mary died of smallpox and Purcell wrote the music for her funeral service.

Purcell died in his mid-thirties. His death has, at various times, been attributed to catching a chill after his wife locked him out, poisoning and tuberculosis. No-one will ever really know for certain. He is buried in Westminster Abbey, London.

GEORGE FRIDERIC HANDEL

18TH-CENTURY GENIUS

BORN Halle,
Saxony-Anhalt
(now Germany),
23 February 1685
DIED London,
14 April 1759
AGE 74 years

George Frideric Handel was born in what is now Germany but moved to London and took British citizenship. His music is some of the best-loved of the 18th century. Beethoven said of him, 'Handel is the greatest composer that ever lived.'

Handel showed musical talent from an early age – he could play the organ and harpsichord when he was seven years old and began to compose music at the age of nine. Although his father wanted the young Handel to become a lawyer, George was allowed to take music lessons with a local organist.

In 1702 Handel began his legal studies but, after his father's death the following year, he abandoned these to study music full-time. He became the organist at

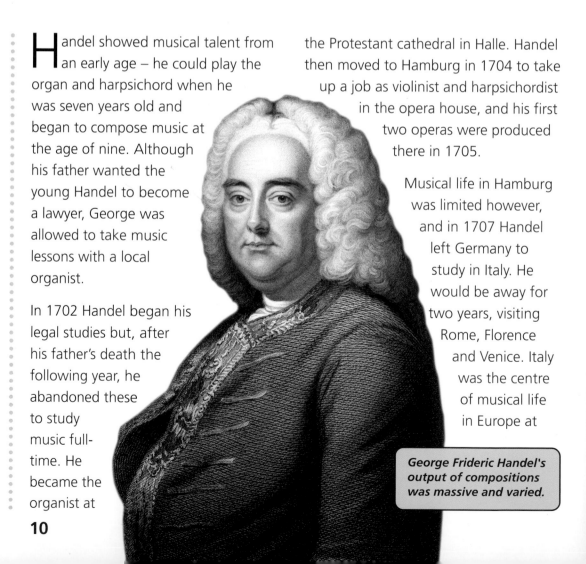

the Protestant cathedral in Halle. Handel then moved to Hamburg in 1704 to take up a job as violinist and harpsichordist in the opera house, and his first two operas were produced there in 1705.

Musical life in Hamburg was limited however, and in 1707 Handel left Germany to study in Italy. He would be away for two years, visiting Rome, Florence and Venice. Italy was the centre of musical life in Europe at

George Frideric Handel's output of compositions was massive and varied.

the time and Handel thrived, writing both religious music and operas.

In 1710 Handel returned to Germany and took a job as *Kapellmeister* (master of religious music) to George, Elector of Hanover, who was to become King George I of Great Britain in 1714. Handel visited London in 1710 and settled there in 1712. He was granted an income of £200 a year from Queen Anne. In the next few years Handel composed some of his best-known works, including the *Water Music*, which was written for a royal party on the River Thames in 1717.

The 1720s and 1730s were a very productive time for Handel. He wrote many operas, which were performed with great success. He also composed chamber music. He became involved in the management of some of the London theatres where his operas were performed, but gave up this activity in the 1730s after he lost money.

In 1727 George I died; Handel was commissioned to write four anthems for the coronation of his son, King George II. One of these, 'Zadok the Priest', has been performed at every coronation since.

By the 1730s, Italian opera was not as popular in London and Handel began composing oratorios. These were stories, mainly from the Bible, set to music with the words in English. Handel's fame

Oratorio

Oratorio usually, though not always, presents a religious story using the same musical elements as opera. It began in Italy in the late 16th century; a distant descendant of the religious plays performed during the Middle Ages. In their early form, oratorios had costumes, scenery and dramatic action, just like operas; in Britain, by the 18th and 19th centuries, oratorios were performed without scenery or costumes.

increased despite a stroke in 1737 which affected his right arm. In 1742 his most famous oratorio, *Messiah*, was premiered in Dublin and then London. Handel started going blind in 1751, and by the time of his death in 1759 he was completely without sight.

Much of Handel's personal life is shrouded in mystery – he was a very private man. He never married, and was generous to charities such as the Foundling Hospital (a hospital in London set up to care for abandoned babies and children). After his death, his oratorios and chamber music continued to be very popular, but his operas were largely forgotten until people started performing them again in the 1960s. Handel remains one of the best-known and best-loved composers that has ever lived.

SIR ARTHUR SULLIVAN
FAMOUS COMPOSER OF COMIC OPERAS

BORN London,
13 May 1842
DIED London,
22 November 1900
AGE 58 years

Arthur Sullivan became a Victorian celebrity through his partnership with the writer W S Gilbert. Together they created some of the world's best-loved comic operas.

Sullivan was born in Lambeth, South London. His father was a military bandmaster, and by the time Arthur was eight years old he could play most of the instruments then used in a military band. Sullivan became a chorister at the Chapel Royal before further studies at London's Royal Academy of Music. Then he went to Leipzig in Germany to study composition (how to write music), returning in 1862.

Sullivan's first musical works were serious in character, and included the Symphony in E of 1866 and the *Festival Te Deum* of 1872. Composing did not, however, provide enough money to live on; he added to his income by working as a church organist and composing hymns, such as the famous 'Onward, Christian Soldiers!' of 1872.

In 1875 the theatrical manager Richard D'Oyly Carte paid Sullivan to write the music for a one-act comic opera, *Trial by Jury*. The librettist (writer of the words)

was W S Gilbert, and a famous partnership had begun. (Sullivan had actually briefly worked with Gilbert as early as 1871 but only on a short Christmas work.) *Trial by Jury* was an instant success.

In 1878 the Gilbert and Sullivan team produced *HMS Pinafore*, which was such a success that it made the pair into Victorian celebrities. *HMS Pinafore* was followed by *The Pirates of Penzance* in 1879 and *Patience* in 1881. Meanwhile D'Oyly Carte had built the New Savoy Theatre, and it was here that their next opera, *Iolanthe*, premiered in 1882. For this reason, the Gilbert and Sullivan collaborations are often known as the 'Savoy' operas.

Sullivan was knighted by Queen Victoria in 1883. He began to feel that his work with Gilbert was unimportant, but it brought him huge financial success. Despite these feelings, in 1882 Sullivan signed a further five-year contract with

Gilbert and D'Oyly Carte. Their next opera, *Princess Ida* (1884), was not such a success, and the partnership seemed to have stalled, but at the last minute the two came up with *The Mikado* in 1885 – their most successful opera.

After *The Mikado* followed *Ruddigore* (1887), *The Yeomen of the Guard* (1888) and *The Gondoliers* (1889). While *The Gondoliers* was playing at the New Savoy Theatre, Gilbert and Sullivan had a serious quarrel, from which the partnership never really recovered. Sullivan, wanting to write serious opera, produced *Ivanhoe* (1891) which was not a success, but worked with Gilbert on two

more comic operas, *Utopia Limited* (1893) and *The Grand Duke* (1896), both of which failed to match the popularity of earlier works.

During the years of his partnership with W S Gilbert, Sullivan continued conducting as well as writing serious compositions, such as *The Golden Legend* (1886). Although a popular concert item until the early 20th century, it was hardly played until recently.

Arthur Sullivan never married but had many romantic affairs. He died from pneumonia at the early age of 58 in 1900. There is a statue of him in the Embankment Gardens near the River Thames, London. 🇬🇧

Arthur Sullivan is remembered for the comic operas that he wrote.

SIR EDWARD ELGAR
BRITAIN'S ROMANTIC GENIUS

BORN Lower
Broadheath,
2 June 1857
DIED Malvern,
23 February 1934
AGE 76 years

For many, the romantic music of Edward Elgar suggests the peace and stability of the early 20th century, when Britain was at the height of its international power. All this was to be shattered by the horrors of World War I.

Edward Elgar was born in the village of Lower Broadheath, outside Worcester. His father, William Elgar, was a piano tuner and music dealer, with a shop in Worcester High Street. Elgar was largely self-taught; being surrounded by musical instruments in his father's shop must have helped. He left school at 15 and worked for a local solicitor, but soon began to teach piano and violin.

At the age of 22, Elgar took the job of bandmaster at the Worcester and County Lunatic Asylum; here he composed as well. He also played the violin in the orchestras of the Worcester and Birmingham festivals. In 1889 Elgar married Alice Roberts, an author, against the wishes of her family. The couple moved to London so that Elgar could compose professionally, but they soon returned to Worcester. By the 1890s, Elgar was becoming well-known as a composer of works for choral festivals,

but in 1899 he had his first great orchestral success – *The Enigma Variations* – which premiered in London. In 1900 his popular choral work, *The Dream of Gerontius,* made its debut at the Birmingham Music Festival. Also from this period is 'Pomp and Circumstance March No. 1', a theme from which became the well-known song 'Land of Hope and Glory'. This is still performed at the last night of the BBC Proms Concerts held at the Royal Albert Hall in London every year.

By 1902 Elgar had become a highly successful and wealthy musician. Knighted in 1904, he was Professor of Music at the University of Birmingham between 1905–08. His Symphony No. 1 (1908) and Symphony No. 2 (1911) were great successes. He was then asked to write a violin concerto (completed in 1910) by the world-famous violinist, Fritz Kreisler, who was the first to play it.

An older Edward Elgar works on a composition, seated at his desk.

During World War I (1914-18), Elgar's music became less popular, and he composed fewer works. Elgar had been deeply saddened by the war and his Cello Concerto of 1920 is more sombre in tone than earlier pieces. Shortly after he finished it, his wife died – a loss Elgar felt for the rest of his life.

In 1924 Elgar was made 'Master of the King's Musick'. He also began to make recordings of his works with various orchestras. One of the most famous recordings is of Elgar conducting the Violin Concerto played by the brilliant young violinist, Yehudi Menuhin. In 1931 Elgar was made a baronet, an hereditary title granted by the king or queen. Edward Elgar died in 1934, having begun work on a third symphony. Although out of fashion for many years, his music is once again popular with orchestras and is enjoyed by thousands today. 🇬🇧

HENRY WOOD
FOUNDER OF THE PROMS

BORN London,
3 March 1869
DIED London,
19 August 1944
AGE 75 years

Conductor, singer, pianist and educator, Henry Wood was skilled in many areas of music. But it is for founding the famous Proms Concerts that he is best-remembered today.

Wood was born in London. His father was an optician but made a living running a model engine shop. Both his parents were fine amateur musicians, and Wood learned to play the organ, piano and violin by the age of 14.

When Wood was 16 he enrolled in London's Royal Academy of Music. Here he studied voice, piano, composition and organ. He intended to become a singing teacher, and indeed he did teach throughout his career. When Wood finished his two-year course of study at the Royal Academy of Music, he found work as an opera conductor. In the early 1890s he collaborated with Arthur Sullivan (see pages 12-13) on his opera, *The Yeoman of the Guard*.

In 1893 Wood was asked to conduct a new series of concerts – the Promenade Concerts – at the Queen's Hall. The manager of the hall, Robert Newman, wanted to introduce concerts to educate members of the public who otherwise wouldn't experience classical music. The first concert took place on 10 August 1895 and Wood conducted music by the German composer Richard Wagner. This was significant because, up until that time, people in Britain had felt that only non-Britons could conduct 'foreign' music. Wood proved them wrong and the Promenade Concerts became an annual feature of British musical life. Wood introduced many new types of music to the concerts and remained in charge of them until 1941. They are still held today, every summer, at the Royal Albert Hall in London. In addition to his work for the Promenade Concerts, Sir Henry Wood (he was knighted in 1911) conducted concerts around Britain and gave his time generously to amateur groups and the student orchestra at the Royal Academy of Music. He introduced women players into orchestras in 1911, and campaigned for higher pay for orchestral musicians.

Sir Henry Wood was a talented conductor who cared passionately about musical life in Britain.

Wood was a workaholic and the strain of doing so much began to affect his health in his later years. He died in London on 19 August 1944, just after the 50th anniversary concert of the Proms. A bronze bust of Sir Henry graces the stage at every BBC Proms concert today.

RALPH VAUGHAN WILLIAMS

TRADITION AND FOLK MUSIC

BORN Down Ampney, Gloucestershire, 12 October 1872
DIED Leith Hill, near Dorking, Surrey, 26 August 1958
AGE 86 years

Ralph Vaughan Williams wrote symphonies and other orchestral pieces as well as songs, operas and many other types of musical compositions. He incorporated folk music into his work and it is partly this that gives many of his compositions their distinctive 'British' quality.

Ralph (pronounced 'Rafe') Vaughan Williams was born in Down Ampney, Gloucestershire, in 1872. His father, Reverand Arthur Vaughan Williams, was the local Church of England vicar. Sadly, Arthur died in 1875 and Ralph's mother, Margaret, took her children to live with her family at Leith Hill, near Dorking in Surrey.

Vaughan Williams was sent to the public school, Charterhouse, to complete his schooling. He also learnt to play the piano and the violin. After leaving school he went to Cambridge University, reading history

Ralph Vaughan Williams in later life. His musical works have become 20th-century classics.

18

and music at Trinity College, then went on to London's Royal Academy of Music where he learned composition with the well-known composer, Hubert Parry (1848–1914).

In the 1890s, Vaughan Williams travelled abroad to study with the composers Max Bruch (1838–1920) in Berlin and Maurice Ravel (1878–1937) in Paris. He returned to Britain and published his first song, 'Linden Lea', in 1905 – the same year that he was invited to conduct at the first Leith Hill Music Festival; something he was to do until 1953.

In 1904 Vaughan Williams became interested in English folk songs, and began to travel around the countryside collecting songs and writing them down. He made collecting trips with his friend and fellow composer Gustav Holst (1874–1934), which resulted in many tunes and words being written down that otherwise might have been forgotten. He incorporated many folk songs into his later compositions. Vaughan Williams was now working as a composer, a lecturer at the Royal Academy of Music and a music editor. His first big success as a composer came in 1909, when he wrote music to accompany *The Wasps,* a play by the Greek writer Aristophanes and, in 1910, conducted his own works *Fantasia on a Theme of Thomas Tallis* and *A Sea Symphony*. He followed these successes with *A London Symphony* in 1914.

Folk music

Folk music – music performed by ordinary people – has always existed. Traditional British folk songs tell stories of love, work and going off to war; often a song was the way for news of a battle or other event to spread throughout the country. Traditional music was passed from singer to singer without being written down; in many cases songs were local to one small area of the country.

Vaughan Williams served with both the Royal Army Medical Corps and the Royal Garrison Artillery during World War I. After the war his musical success continued; the style of his music changed from the gentle approach of the 'Pastoral' Symphony No. 3 to the vigorous rhythms and clashing harmonies of Symphony No. 4 of 1935.

Vaughan Williams continued to compose during World War II (1939–45); his Symphony No. 5 premiered at the Proms in 1943. He composed his *Serenade to Music* (1938) as a tribute to Sir Henry Wood (see pages 16-17). In the last years of his life Vaughan Williams wrote four more symphonies and many other orchestral and choral works. He died in 1958 and was buried in Westminster Abbey, survived by his second wife Ursula, who wrote his biography.

NOEL COWARD
'THE MASTER'

BORN Teddington,
Middlesex,
16 December 1899
DIED Jamaica,
26 March 1973
AGE 73 years

Noel Coward was born at the turn of the 20th century and was one of the leading all-round men of the theatre of his generation. Actor, playwright, director, composer and popular performer – he thoroughly deserved the nickname by which he was, and still is, universally known: 'The Master'.

Pushed on to the stage by his ambitious mother, Coward made his debut when he was just 11, in the title role of a play called *The Goldfish*. A year later he played Smee in *Peter Pan*. When he was 17, he made his screen debut in a film called *Hearts of the World*. In 1923, Coward started his song-writing career with a revue, *London Calling*, which featured a young American called Fred Astaire. The following year, Coward had his first major success as a playwright with *The Vortex*. He then penned the revue *On With The Dance* for which he composed one of his most famous songs, 'Poor Little Rich Girl'. During the late 1920s and 1930s, there was almost always a Noel Coward play on the stage in London and New York. Songs poured from his pen. For *Cavalcade* he wrote the world-weary '20th Century Blues'. His revue *Words*

Ivor Novello

IVOR NOVELLO (1893–1951) was one of Coward's greatest but friendly rivals. The shows he wrote and appeared in, *Glamorous Nights* (1935), *The Dancing Years* (1939) and *King Rhapsody* (1949) among them, were noted for their lavish sets, large casts and lilting melodies. Two of the songs he wrote became especially famous. 'Keep The Home Fires Burning' (1914) was written at the outbreak of World War I: 'We'll Gather Lilacs In The Spring Again' (1945) when World War II was drawing to an end. He died in 1951. A few years later the Novello Awards were established in his memory, highly prized by all those who write popular music.

This photograph of talented musician, Noel Coward, captures his impish sense of fun.

and Music featured the song 'Mad About The Boy'. These and the other songs he wrote were played in ballrooms and dance halls, hummed by young ladies and whistled by milk boys. Coward also wrote an operetta, *Bitter Sweet* (1929), which contains two of his most popular songs, the lilting 'I'll See You Again' and the wistful 'A Talent To Amuse'.

Noel Coward was knighted in 1970. Three years later, after appearing at a gala performance of the revue *Oh Coward!* in New York, he returned to his home in Jamaica where he died shortly afterwards.

In 1998, Sting, Robbie Williams, Shola Ama, The Divine Comedy and Elton John were among those who sang Coward songs on the album 'Twentieth Century Blues'. The album proved, if proof was needed, that when it came to writing songs with enduring appeal, Noel Coward was indeed 'The Master'. 🏴

MICHAEL TIPPETT
A 20TH-CENTURY MUSICAL GENIUS

BORN London,
2 January 1905
DIED London,
8 January 1998
AGE 93 years

Most composers depend on others to write the words that accompany their music. Not Michael Tippett. He wrote the librettos (words) and music for his operas and oratorios. Along with Benjamin Britten and William Walton, he is one of the highest regarded of 20th-century English composers.

Like many other famous British musicians, Tippett was a student at London's Royal College of Music. As well as studying composition and the piano, he also took courses in conducting with Adrian Boult and Malcolm Sargent, two of the most famous British conductors. This gave him a deep understanding of all aspects of the orchestra.

After he graduated he held several positions as a teacher and conductor, but it was as a composer that he was to make his mark. He wrote five operas, *The Midsummer Marriage* (1955), *King Priam* (1962), *The Knot Garden* (1970), *The Ice Break* (1977) and *New Year* (1988). Even today, they are too 'modern' for many opera-lovers to enjoy but, to music critics, they are milestones in 20th-century opera.

Perhaps his most famous work reflects his lifelong anti-war feelings. They were

Peter Maxwell Davies

PETER MAXWELL DAVIES (b. 1934) is well known as a composer who is unafraid of exploring new musical forms and mixing them with more traditional ones. He has written operas, including *Taverner* (1970), symphonies, song cycles such as *Eight Songs for a Mad King* (1969) and chamber music. In 1970 he moved from England to the Orkney Islands. Since then he has written more lyrical music than before. He is associate conductor/composer with the Royal Philharmonic and BBC Philharmonic orchestras. He was appointed Master of the Queen's Music in 2004.

Sir Michael Tippett was a talented conductor as well as a great British composer.

so strong that he went to jail for three months in 1943 rather than undertake the sort of tasks that were normally given to conscientious objectors during World War II. The piece, an oratorio called *A Child of Our Time*, was first heard in public in 1941. It was inspired by Henshel Grynsban, a Jewish boy who assassinated a member of the German Embassy in Paris in 1938. The work caused a sensation, and remains one of the most important pieces of choral music of the 20th century.

Tippett's musical works include symphonies, piano sonatas, string quartets, a concerto for double string orchestras, music for piano and orchestra, pieces for percussion instruments, a fanfare for trumpets, a suite written to commemorate the birth of Prince Charles in 1948 and many others. He also travelled the world as a conductor and continued to compose into his nineties.

BENJAMIN BRITTEN
THE FIRST COMPOSER TO BE MADE A LORD

BORN Lowestoft,
Suffolk,
22 November, 1913
DIED Aldeburgh,
Suffolk,
4 December, 1976
AGE 63 years

Operas, choral and orchestral works, song cycles, string quartets and other chamber music – Benjamin Britten wrote them all. He was perhaps the most prolific British composer of the 20th century, and one of the greatest.

Benjamin Britten, pictured in front of the Suffolk marshes close to where he lived and worked.

By the time he was 12, Britten had already written an oratorio for children and several string quartets. When he graduated from London's Royal College of Music, he wrote film music and began to attract attention as a serious composer.

In 1939, Britten sailed for the United States where he composed many superb songs and his first stage work, *Paul Bunyan* (1941), about the legendary American hero who carved the Grand Canyon. He returned to Britain in 1943. His deeply held anti-war feelings were expressed in his *War Requiem*. First performed in 1961, it includes musical settings of poems by Wilfred Owen, the famous World War I poet.

By then, Britten had made his mark as the finest composer of modern opera in Britain. *Peter Grimes*, first performed in 1945, is a grim dark story of a suspected child murderer, based in his native Suffolk. By contrast, *Albert Herring* (1947) is a delightful story of a Suffolk man who is elected May Queen, as there are no suitable female candidates. He also wrote operas based on books by Herman Melville (*Billy Budd* – 1951) and Henry James (*The Turn of the Screw* – 1954), and William Shakespeare's play (*Midsummer Night's Dream* – 1960), among others.

Britten enjoyed writing for children – his *The Little Sweep* (or *Let's Make an Opera*) (1949) and *The Young Person's*

Sir William Walton

WILLIAM WALTON (1902–83) shot to fame in 1923 when *Façade*, a musical setting of poems by Edith Sitwell, caused a furore at its premier. He was soon regarded as one of Britain's best composers. His choral work *Belshazzar's Feast* (1931) and his Symphony No. 1 (1934) were performed to huge acclaim. He also wrote operas, *Troilus and Cressida* (1934) and *The Bear* (1967), a ballet – *The Wise Virgins* (1940), chamber and church music, several concertos and much more. During World War II he began to write film music, and was recognised as a master of the art, particularly the themes he wrote for *Henry V*, *Hamlet* and *Richard III*.

Guide to the Orchestra (1946) are perfect introductions to classical music for young children.

Britten, an excellent pianist and superb conductor, spent much of his later life in Suffolk, enjoying the companionship of his long-time partner, the tenor Peter Pears (1910–1986). It was for Pears that Britten wrote many fine vocal works and opera roles, including the lead in his final opera, *Death in Venice* (1973). Much of what Britten wrote was first performed at The Maltings, the concert hall he had built at Snape, Suffolk. The annual festival there is a magnet for serious music lovers from all over the world. 🇬🇧

VERA LYNN
THE FORCES' SWEETHEART

BORN London,
20 March 1917

In 1995, to mark the 50th anniversary of the ending of World War II in Europe, the Queen, the Queen Mother and Princess Margaret, appeared on the balcony of Buckingham Palace. Among the singers chosen to entertain them was Vera Lynn. When she sang, nostalgic tears filled the eyes of the thousands of ex-servicemen in the crowd.

From her early childhood it was clear that Vera Lynn had a remarkable singing voice. By the time she was seven she was performing in working men's clubs, and in 1935, she made her debut on the radio with a popular dance band.

In 1940, in the early days of World War II, Vera Lynn launched herself on a solo career and was soon given her own radio show on the BBC, 'Sincerely Yours'. The show was a musical link between soldiers and other servicemen overseas and their girls 'back home'. Lynn read out messages and sang songs, such as 'We'll Meet Again', which was to become her signature tune.

Within a year she had established herself as the most popular female vocalist in Britain and with servicemen overseas, and was widely known as 'the forces'

Kathleen Ferrier

Lancashire-born **KATHLEEN FERRIER** (1912–53) was working as a telephonist when she entered a singing competition in 1940. Her rich contralto voice earned her first prize, and encouraged by her success she decided to study singing seriously. She was quickly recognised by both critics and audiences as having not just a remarkable voice, but extraordinary vocal control. In 1946 she created the title role in Benjamin Britten's opera *The Rape of Lucretia* and from then on was in constant demand in Europe and the USA. Her early death from breast cancer in 1953 robbed the musical world of one of its greatest talents. But we can still enjoy her exquisite voice thanks to the recordings she made.

Vera Lynn makes a recording. Her voice became loved by thousands during World War II.

sweetheart'. As the war continued, she appeared in several films and even flew to Burma (now Myanmar) to entertain the troops stationed there.

After the war, with variety theatres (music-halls) in decline, Lynn concentrated on her recording, radio and television career, singing the songs with which she was most associated. But she was not afraid to record new material, including the Gene Pitney hit 'By The Time I Get To Phoenix' and The Beatles' song 'Fool On The Hill' from their 'Revolver' album.

Vera Lynn was awarded an OBE in 1970 and was promoted to Dame five years after that. Since then she has kept her appearances more or less restricted to events organised to commemorate significant events of World War II where, to many of those in the audience who served in the armed forces, she remains their 'sweetheart'.

JOHN DANKWORTH
AND CLEO LAINE
THE ROYAL COUPLE OF BRITISH JAZZ

JOHN DANKWORTH:
BORN London,
20 September 1927
CLEO LAINE:
BORN Southall,
Middlesex,
18 October 1927

It is impossible to think of either Laine or Dankworth without the other coming to mind, so famous are they as a couple. But John Dankworth and Cleo Laine are jazz legends in their own rights.

John Dankworth started playing the clarinet when he was a child and later studied at London's Royal Academy of Music. After graduating, he went to New York where he played with jazz legend Charlie Parker (1920–1955) who encouraged Dankworth to switch from clarinet to alto saxophone.

Back in London, Dankworth founded the Johnny Dankworth Seven in 1950. Three years later he formed a big band to play his own arrangements of music standards. Among those who auditioned to sing with the band was Cleo Laine. Her unique voice, bluesy and smoky in the lower octaves, rising to an almost piercing but pure shrill the higher it goes, got her the job. The couple married in 1958 and have become Britain's best known and best loved jazz partnership.

The big band provided the perfect vehicle for Dankworth's skills as an

Richard Rodney Bennett

RICHARD RODNEY BENNETT (b. 1936) was born into a musical family and began writing music when he was a child. Today he is better known as a jazz pianist, cabaret singer and composer of film music. The score he wrote for *Murder on the Orient Express* (1974) included a delightful waltz, which is the piece he is most often asked to play. He also wrote the original music for the film *Four Weddings and a Funeral* (1994). In 2006, he composed *Reflections on a Scottish Folk Song*, a piece for cello and string orchestra, in memory of Queen Elizabeth the Queen Mother, commissioned by the Prince of Wales.

arranger and saxophonist, but his talents extend far beyond that. He has written classical music, including *Fair Oak Fusions,* a nine-movement piece written for and recorded by cellist Julian Lloyd Webber, as well as collaborating with violinist Yehudi Menuhin, flautist James Galway and pop idol Craig David.

Laine, meanwhile, has continued her career under the musical direction of her husband. She has been compared to Ella Fitzgerald and Sarah Vaughan, regarded as America's two greatest jazz singers. Her recording of George Gershwin's *Porgy and Bess* with Ray Charles, is regarded as a classic. She has also made albums with flautist James Galway and guitarist John Williams, recorded jazz versions of lyrics by Shakespeare, W H Auden, T S Eliot and Thomas Hardy and works by Kurt Weill and Arnold Schoenberg.

Laine and Dankworth's interest in musical education led them to found the Wavendon Allmusic Plan and to build a performing centre at their home in Wavendon. The centre attracts stars from around the world, who play for and lecture jazz enthusiasts who flock to the workshops and courses organised by the 'royal couple of British jazz'.

Cleo Laine and John Dankworth are two of Britain's best-known jazz musicians.

JACQUELINE DU PRÉ
BRITAIN'S GREATEST-EVER CELLIST

BORN Oxford,
26 January, 1945
DIED London,
19 October, 1987
AGE 42 years

Jacqueline du Pré was hailed as a brilliant cellist when she was still a child. She enjoyed a dazzling career in both the concert hall and recording studio: a career that was tragically cut short when she was struck down by an incurable illness.

Jacqueline du Pré, aged about 25, with her cello. Her tragic illness robbed the musical world of a great talent.

One day in 1949, four-year-old Jacqueline du Pré heard a cello on the radio. 'Mummy,' she said, 'I want to make a sound like that.' A few weeks later, on her fifth birthday, she awoke to find a child-size cello at the foot of her bed. Lessons showed she had an extraordinary talent for it.

In 1956, as soon as Sir John Barbirolli, one of England's greatest conductors, heard her play for an important scholarship, he knew immediately she was the winner. She played her first concert a year later, and in 1958 began to study Elgar's Cello Concerto (see page 15), the piece of music that was to become most associated with her.

In 1961, she made her professional solo debut in London's Wigmore Hall, playing a cello made in 1673 by the famous instrument maker, Antonio Stradivarius. The priceless cello was a gift from an anonymous admirer! A year later she played the Elgar concerto at her first professional concert with an orchestra. It was a triumph, but at just 17 she started to doubt herself and refused concert engagements for a while. She was coaxed back to work when whoever had given her the 1673 Stradivarius cello offered to buy her an even better one. When she played the Elgar concerto with it in New York in 1965 she was given a ten-minute standing ovation.

In 1966 du Pré married the young Israeli pianist and conductor, Daniel Barenboim

Lionel Tertis

Very few people have heard the name **LIONEL TERTIS** (1876–1975), but he was one of Britain's greatest musicians. After studying piano and violin, he started to play the viola at the age of 19. Tertis arranged many works for the viola, including Edward Elgar's Cello Concerto, Frederick Delius's violin sonatas and Johannes Brahms's clarinet works. It was Tertis who persuaded Sir William Walton (see page 25) to write his beautiful Viola Concerto, which brought the instrument to the attention of other composers, including Ralph Vaughan Williams (see pages 18–19) and Benjamin Britten (see pages 24–25). When he died, he was recognised around the world as the man who had rescued the viola from musical obscurity.

(b. 1942). They became the golden couple of the music world. With Barenboim conducting, his wife played all the great cello pieces. But in 1972 she noticed that a numb feeling in her hand that she had first noticed eight years before was getting worse.

In 1973, she was diagnosed with multiple sclerosis, an incurable disease that eventually left her helpless and wheelchair-bound. She died in 1987 aged just 42, one of the greatest cello players the world has ever known.

ERIC CLAPTON
'THE BEST WHITE BLUES GUITARIST'

BORN Ripley, Surrey, 30 March, 1945

Eric Clapton has played guitar with two of the most influential British bands. Universally regarded as the most outstanding white blues guitarist in the world, his career has been one of exceptional musical achievement marred by personal tragedy.

Clapton was brought up by his grandparents. At the age of 14 he was given his first guitar which he practised endlessly, playing along to records of the great rock, R&B (rhythm and blues) and blues guitarists.

In 1963 he joined The Yardbirds, an R&B band. Clapton left after two years to play first with Bluesbreakers, the band led by John Mayall (b. 1933), and later, in 1966, to join Cream with drummer Ginger Baker (b. 1939) and bass player Jack Bruce (b. 1943). They made three stunning albums, 'Fresh Cream' (1966), 'Disraeli Gears' (1967) and 'Wheels on Fire' (1968) before the band split up.

In 1970, Clapton released his first solo album, 'Eric Clapton'. In the same year he recorded 'Layla' with his band, Derek and the Dominos. It is considered by many to be one of the best rock singles of all time. But by now he was in the grip of a serious heroin addiction, which brought his public appearances to a halt.

David Bowie

DAVID BOWIE (b. 1947) had a minor hit in 1969 with his record 'Space Oddity' which roughly coincided with the first moon landing. In 1972 he came to big-time fame as the outrageous glam-rocker Ziggy Stardust. The album 'The Rise and Fall of Ziggy Stardust and the Spiders from Mars' gave Bowie his first million-selling album. For the next eight years Bowie was rarely out of the charts. His concert tours sold out as soon as they were announced, all over the world. In the mid-1970s he went to live in Berlin where, with **BRIAN ENO** (b. 1949), he made three albums, including 'Heroes' (1977) which is reckoned to be Bowie's best.

In 1973, Pete Townshend (b. 1945) of The Who coaxed him back for an all-star London concert. Boosted by its success, Clapton sought treatment for his addiction and his career was successfully relaunched resulting in ground-breaking albums such as 'Slowhand' (1977) and 'Backless' (1978). But his heroin addiction had been replaced by a serious alcohol problem that forced him to take treatment in 1981.

In 1991 his four-year-old son, Conor, fell from a New York City apartment block and died. The song Clapton wrote about the tragedy, 'Tears in Heaven', was a massive hit. It won a Grammy Award (one of the music industry's highest awards). Clapton has won, or shared in, 18 Grammies in total.

In 2005 Clapton, Bruce and Baker re-formed Cream to play a few successful reunion concerts. Since then, Clapton continues to tour and record albums. 🇬🇧

Eric Clapton performs guitar on stage. He is widely held to be the best blues guitarist ever.

ANDREW LLOYD WEBBER
LORD OF THE WEST END MUSICAL

BORN London,
22 March 1948

Andrew Lloyd Webber is the most successful composer of West End musicals in history. His shows have broken box-office records in London, on Broadway and in many other countries. His songs have been recorded by some of the most famous pop and classical singers.

Andrew Lloyd Webber's father was a music professor and his mother a talented pianist. During his first year at Oxford University, Lloyd Webber wrote the music for a show with lyrics by fellow student Tim Rice. The second show they wrote, *Joseph and the Amazing Technicolor Dreamcoat* (1967), was their first hit.

Then came *Jesus Christ Superstar* (1971). With its mix of heavy rock numbers, sentimental ballads and witty takes on other musical styles, the show was a smash hit.

In 1975, Lloyd Webber had a flop with *By Jeeves*. But a year later he and Rice had another major success with *Evita*, a musical biography of Eva, wife of the Argentinean dictator, Juan Peron.

Lloyd Webber's taste for unconventional themes for his musicals was seen again in his next show, *Cats* (1981). Based on T S Eliot's poetry collection *Old Possum's*

Book of Practical Cats, the show ran in London for 21 years in London and in 1997 became the longest running show in the history of Broadway.

Lionel Bart

Jesus Christ Superstar opened in London the same year that *Oliver* by **LIONEL BART** (1930–1999) was revived. Based on Charles Dickens' novel *Oliver Twist*, it is the story of an orphan boy who is forced to pick pockets for an evil miser, Fagin. The show first opened in June 1960 and ran for 2,618 performances. Bart had already written several pop songs including Cliff Richard's hit, 'Livin' Doll' and another musical, *Fings Ain't Wot They Used T'Be* (1960). He went on to write more musicals, but none matched *Oliver*, which became a film in 1968 and won several Oscars, including Best Picture.

Since then he has written *Song and Dance* (1982), *Starlight Express* (1984) – with the cast on rollerskates, *Phantom of the Opera* (1986), *Aspects of Love* (1989) and *Sunset Boulevard* (1993). When that show opened on Broadway in New York it had advance box office takings of a record-breaking $37.5 million. It was followed by the less successful *Whistle Down the Wind* (1996) and *Woman in White* (2003), based on the Wilkie Collins novel.

Lloyd Webber has also written for the cinema, and his arrangement of Paganini's 'Variations' for cello brought his brother, Julian, major success. The requiem he wrote in 1985 stands comparison with more seriously regarded religious music.

Andrew Lloyd Webber was knighted in 1992 and made a lord in 1997.

> **Andrew Lloyd Webber's musicals, seen by millions, have made him a fortune and earned him a peerage.**

ELVIS COSTELLO
'THE MAIN ATTRACTION'

BORN London,
25 August 1954

Singer/songwriter Elvis Costello has been at the top of the popular music scene for 30 years. As guitar/vocalist with The Attractions, and even more successfully as a songwriter, he has explored all aspects of music from jazz to classical.

Born Declan MacManus, his father worked as a jazz musician. When his parents divorced, Declan and his mother moved to Liverpool. A few years later, it was in Liverpool that he went to hear a singer called Nick Lowe. Inspired by Lowe, MacManus, who was working as a computer operator with a London cosmetic company, formed his own band, Flip City. While continuing to work as a computer operator, MacManus recorded some solo songs and sent demonstration tapes to various record companies. Finally, in 1976, Nick Lowe at Stiff Records signed him up. At this point MacManus took on the stage name, Elvis Costello, by which he was to become known on stage and off. The following year he joined other musicians to form Elvis Costello and the Attractions. They have made many successful albums and concert tours.

Elton John

ELTON JOHN (b. 1947) has been at the top of the popular musical world for over five decades as a singer and songwriter. His first album, 'Empty Sky' (1969) made little impact. But later the same year his second, 'Elton John', was a hit in the UK and US, the first of many. He has written the music for several Disney films, most notably *The Lion King* (with Tim Rice), which sold more than 15 million albums. In 1997, he sang a rewritten version of his hit 'Candle In The Wind' from his 1973 album 'Goodbye Yellow Brick Road' at the funeral of Diana, Princess of Wales. It went on to sell 30 million copies, making £55 million for the Princess's Memorial Fund.

The range of singers and musicians who have recorded Elvis Costello songs includes Chet Baker, Johnny Cash, Roy Orbison, Dusty Springfield and others. He has collaborated with other songwriters including America's Burt Baccarach, Swedish singer Anne Sofie von Otter and most recently with the jazz pianist and singer Diana Krall, who is also his wife.

Elvis Costello, wearing his trademark black-framed glasses, is a modern musical genius.

In 2004 'The Scarlet Tide', the song he wrote for the film *Cold Mountain,* was nominated for an Oscar. After the devastation caused by Hurricane Katrina in 2006, Costello played two benefit concerts in New Orleans to raise money for the victims. There, he played with Allen Toussaint, a legendary piano player, songwriter and producer who hails from that city. The two musicians later collaborated on the album 'The River in Reverse' which was released to rave reviews later in the year.

Magnetic performer, acclaimed songwriter, Elvis Costello is one of the most talented musicians of his generation.

SIMON RATTLE
THE GLAMOUR MAN OF BRITISH CONDUCTING

BORN Liverpool,
19 January 1955

Born in Liverpool five or six years before it became the centre of the pop world, Simon Rattle's musical taste took him in a different direction, into the world of classical music. At an age when most conductors were still struggling to launch their careers, Rattle was wielding his baton in front of many of the world's greatest orchestras.

When Simon Rattle was a child, he enjoyed putting on concerts at which he conducted as friends and relatives played their instruments. Still a schoolboy, he became conductor of the Merseyside Youth Orchestra, where he conducted music by Igor Stravinsky (1882–1971), Benjamin Britten (see pages 24–25), Michael Tippett (see pages 22–23) and many others. His school days over, he headed to London's Royal Academy of Music where, in 1974, he won first prize in the John Player International Conducting Competition. When he graduated, he was appointed Assistant Conductor of the Bournemouth Symphony Orchestra.

Taking up the baton

Simon Rattle is the latest in a long line of British conductors who reached the top of their career. **SIR THOMAS BEECHAM** (1879–1961) had a long conducting career and founded the Royal Philharmonic Orchestra. His near contemporary, **SIR JOHN BARBIROLLI** (1899–1970), trained as a cellist before becoming a conductor. Under his direction, Manchester's Halle Orchestra came to be regarded as one of the best in the world, especially renowned for promoting the works of modern composers. **SIR MALCOLM SARGENT** (1895–1967) was in charge of the Liverpool Symphony (1942–48) and BBC Symphony (1950–57) orchestras. He was especially noted for choral music and for being perhaps the most popular conductor at the Last Night of the Proms Concert in London.

Sir Simon Rattle conducts a rehearsal. His appointment as conductor of the Berlin Philharmonic was remarkable as he was only 44 years old.

With his mop of curly hair and his pop-star looks, he quickly established himself as a concert-hall favourite. But it takes more than that to impress serious music lovers and, more importantly, musicians. That takes dedication, genuine talent and a deep, instinctive love of music. Rattle has it all.

In 1977, he became the youngest-ever conductor to appear at the Proms (see page 16) and two years later he made his North American debut with the Los Angeles Philharmonic Orchestra. In 1980 he was appointed chief conductor with the City of Birmingham Symphony Orchestra. During his years there he conducted 934 concerts and rehearsed for over 10,000 hours, turning it into one of the best in Britain. Somehow he found the time to appear as guest conductor with many of the world's highest regarded orchestras. After 20 years in Birmingham, he was appointed conductor of the Berlin Philharmonic, a unique honour for a man of just 44.

Equally at home conducting for the opera as he is in the concert hall, Rattle is as brilliant at conducting music by 20th century composers as he is with earlier ones like Mozart, Beethoven and Mahler.

THE BEATLES
THE 'FAB FOUR'

FIRST APPEARANCE
Hamburg, West Germany,
17 September, 1960
FORMAL SPLIT London,
10 April, 1970

The Beatles hit the pop world at the beginning of the 'swinging sixties' and dominated it for the rest of the decade. Today, every minute of every day, somewhere in the world a radio station is playing one of their tracks. They were, and always will be, one of the greatest groups in history.

The 'Fab Four', pictured in 1966. From left, Ringo Starr, Paul McCartney, George Harrison and John Lennon.

The Swinging Sixties

The success of The Beatles helped launch 'The Mersey Sound' – groups such as Gerry and the Pacemakers, Billy J. Kramer and the Dakotas and others, often singing songs created by Lennon and McCartney. They appealed as much to parents as they did to teenagers. Not so with bands such as The Rolling Stones and The Who, whose throbbing rock music influenced by American rhythm and blues was, to adult ears, too loud and too discordant to be called 'music'. Youngsters with rebellion on their mind disagreed. For a decade or more, they swung to The Rolling Stones and the like while others swung to The Beatles and their imitators. No wonder the decade was called 'The Swinging Sixties'.

In August 1962, the drummer in a Liverpool band called The Beatles was replaced by Ringo Starr (b. 1940). With fellow musicians, John Lennon (1940–80), Paul McCartney (b. 1942) and George Harrison (1942–2001), he became part of a pop legend. Their first single, 'Love Me Do', was released in September 1962. Their second, 'Please Please Me' (January 1963) was the first of 12 chart-toppers. Their debut album, 'Please Please Me' (May 1963), was the best-seller for 30 weeks until it was replaced by their second, 'With The Beatles'. The mass hysteria the band generated wherever they appeared, at home or abroad, was reflected in their first movie, *A Hard Day's Night* (1964).

Successive albums saw the band mature from the 'yeah, yeah' of 'pop rock' to more philosophical material such as 'In My Life', tender love songs including McCartney's 'Yesterday' and the psychedelically influenced 'Strawberry Fields For Ever'. Drug-inspired psychedelics were at the heart of rock's first concept album, 'Sgt Pepper's Lonely Hearts Club Band' (1967), which topped the charts for 22 weeks. By this time the band had given up touring to concentrate on recording. In 1968 they set up their own recording company and released 'Hey Jude', which sold six million copies – their best-selling single. More albums followed including 'Abbey Road', with its sleeve showing the 'Fab Four' on the zebra crossing outside the Abbey Road music studios.

In April 1970, McCartney announced he was splitting from the others. Talk of a reunion was finally quashed when Lennon was murdered in New York in 1980. Harrison died of cancer in 2001, by which time Starr had faded from the pop scene. McCartney continues to write, record and appear in concert, the last performing member of one of the greatest bands in history.

COURTNEY PINE
A MAN WITH A MISSION

BORN London,
18 March 1964

A dazzling performer on saxophone, clarinet, flute and keyboards, Courtney Pine moved from reggae and funk into the world of jazz. His music is amongst the most interesting on the British jazz scene.

Courtney Pine was given a recorder when he was nine and went on to learn several musical instruments. By the age of 16 he had decided that he wanted to be a professional musician.

He played with Dwarf Steps, a hard-bop band, and for reggae stars Clint

Jazz

Jazz – Afro-American folk music influenced by the popular European music of the day – was first played, in the United States, around 1900. In the beginning, it was centred in New Orleans, but by 1925 it had spread to New York and had reached Europe. Jazz players take the basic tune and improvise on it in their own style, taking it in turns to take the lead. 'Modern jazz' began in the 1960s, when players such as Miles Davis took improvisation to new levels, often leaving the original melody far behind.

Eastwood and General Saint. Then, in the mid-1980s, he attended workshops run by one of the leaders of the London jazz scene, John Stevens. This led to Pine setting up Jazz Warriors, a band that played to small but enthusiastic audiences in and around London.

He came to wider public attention when he appeared with the Charlie Watts Orchestra and other jazz bands, and featured at the Camden Jazz Festival in 1986. A year later, he played at the Bath Festival with the Orchestre National de Jazz, by which time his reputation had spread far beyond smoky jazz clubs.

Pine's first album, 'Journey To The Urge Within', made it to the UK's 'Top 40', a huge achievement for a jazz musician. He came to mainstream fame when he appeared at the concert held at Wembley Stadium to mark Nelson Mandela's 70th birthday in 1988 and since then he has been one of *the* faces of British jazz.

His television and radio shows appeal to

audiences who have never given jazz a chance until they hear one of his programmes.

Pine has continued to test the boundaries of jazz, often fusing it with reggae and hip-hop. His achievements were recognised with an OBE in 2000, a Fellowship to the Leeds College of

Music and, in 2005, an honorary doctorate of music from the University of Westminster. He continues to perform and record and gives workshops in schools. 🇬🇧

Courtney Pine, pictured in 2000. He is one of Britain's most innovative jazz performers.

EVELYN GLENNIE
A DRUMMER WHO HAPPENS TO BE DEAF

BORN Aberdeen,
19 July 1965

To become an internationally famous musician is a rare achievement. To do so as a profoundly deaf drummer is unique. Yet that is exactly what Scots-born Evelyn Glennie has done. Refusing to be described as 'a deaf drummer', she prefers to be called, 'a drummer who happens to be deaf.'

Evelyn Glennie grew up in a family that made its own music: her mother at the piano, her father on the accordion and Evelyn and the others singing along. Her piano teacher was quick to spot that her eight-year-old pupil had perfect pitch – the ability to sing or play any note after hearing it once. Sadly, Evelyn noticed that her hearing was becoming duller, and by the time she was 12 she was recognised as being profoundly deaf. She was fitted with a hearing aid but soon got rid of it as she said it distorted sound. Amazingly her deafness did nothing to dampen her ambition to become a professional percussionist. When drums and the other percussion instruments are hit, they send out sound waves or reverberations. By feeling these in her body, Evelyn Glennie knows the precise note the instrument is making. And by knowing how to make them produce these reverberations, she can create the sounds that she wants.

The boys at the back

Drummers usually stand or sit at the back of the orchestra or are the least-known members of a pop group. There are exceptions. **GINGER BAKER** (see page 32) played with the groups Cream and Blind Faith and is one of the best-known rock drummers in the business. **RINGO STARR** (see page 41) was as famous as the other Beatles: so is **CHARLIE WATTS** (b. 1941) of the Rolling Stones. But the only drummer to go from the back to stardom as a solo singer is **PHIL COLLINS** (b. 1951). As drummer with Genesis, Collins was already famous when, in 1981, he released his first solo album, 'Face Value'. Collins has also won an Oscar for the song that he wrote for the Disney film *Tarzan*.

Evelyn Glennie poses with a large gong. She has raised the profile of percussionists in the musical world.

When she applied for a place at London's Royal Academy of Music, staff were so doubtful of her ability that they made her audition twice. Evelyn excelled in her studies at the Academy and went on to make her London debut at the Wigmore Hall in 1986.

Today, she has played with all the major orchestras. In concerts she frequently removes her shoes so she can 'feel' the music through her lower body as well as through her hands. Her interest in music extends to rock and pop, having collaborated with such pop stars as Sting, Ray Davies and Björk. She is also a gifted composer and has written and recorded a number of songs.

Glossary

Album One or more pieces of recorded music, usually by the same musical artist, or group. A concept album has songs linked by a common theme.

Anthem A musical setting of religious words, usually sung by the choir in a church; or a morale-boosting, patriotic song, such as 'God Save the Queen'.

Aria A song sung by a soloist in an opera.

Arrangement The way a piece of music is adapted to be played by the various instruments in an orchestra or band.

Ballad A song that tells a story and which usually has a chorus, repeated between verses.

Bandmaster The leader and conductor of a band, usually a military band or marching band.

Big band A large jazz or dance band that plays popular music, usually without any stringed instruments.

Blues Folk music that originated among Afro-Americans at the start of the 20th century. Blues music is often about being unhappy with life in general, or with love in particular.

Box-office The small room in a theatre or concert hall from where tickets are sold. A box-office hit is a show that takes lots of money in ticket sales.

Broadway The theatre area in Manhattan, New York, around Times Square where many of the city's most successful plays and musicals are staged.

Chamber music Music written to be played by a trio, quartet or other small group of musicians.

Chorister A singer in a choir, especially a choirboy or choirgirl.

Chorus This has several meanings for musicians. It can be a number of singers who sing together: a refrain in which others, such as audience members, join a soloist in a song: a line or group of lines repeated at intervals in a song: or a solo section based on the main melody of a popular song and played by a member of the group.

Concerto A musical composition written for one or two soloists to perform accompanied by a large orchestra.

Conductor The musician who faces the musicians in an orchestra, signalling when they should start and finish playing and how they should play – as required by the composer.

Festival A programme of cultural performances, exhibitions, or competitions often held over the course of a few days, such as the Malvern Festival.

Folk music Music, often unaccompanied songs, that started among the working-class people of a nation or region and spread about or passed down orally from generation to generation.

Funk A style of music that came out of jazz and blues in the 1960s and 1970s and which has a strong rhythm.

Hard-bop Fast rhythmic dance music in a jazz style that evolved in the 1950s and 1960s.

Libretto The words in an opera, written to be sung. The word comes from the Italian *libro* which means 'book'.

Liturgy Music written for regular performance during religious worship, such as the chants sung by monks at regular times of each day.

Lyrics The words of a popular song.

Motet A composition, usually based on a sacred text and sung without accompaniment, in which the individual singers sing separate melodies that harmonise with each other.

Musical A show, such as *The Phantom of the Opera* or *The Sound of Music* that tells a story in words and song.

Ode Strictly speaking, an ode is a lyric poem, usually dedicated to a particular person or thing, but several composers have called pieces odes, such as Handel who wrote 'An Ode for St Cecilia' in 1739.

Opera A dramatic performance which is set to music.

Oratorio A musical composition for voices and orchestra, telling a sacred story without costumes, scenery or dramatic action, such as Handel's *Messiah*, which tells the story of the life of Christ.

Percussion instruments Instruments that are shaken, like tambourines, or struck, like drums, to produce a noise.

Premier The first public performance of a play or piece of musical theatre.

Reggae Jolly, jerky music that started in the West Indies, with a rhythm that encourages people to dance to it.

Requiem A musical setting of the Roman Catholic service for the dead.

Sonata A piece written for one or more solo instruments, one of which is usually a keyboard instrument.

Song cycle A group of songs written to be performed one after the other.

Standard A song that has been recorded by several singers over the years and which retains its popularity regardless of how it is performed.

Suite An instrumental composition, especially popular in the 17th and 18th centuries, consisting of a series of different pieces linked by a common theme, such as music to be danced to.

Symphony A long piece of music in three or more movements written to be played by a full orchestra.

Vocalist A singer, usually with a big band or rock group.

Some useful websites

www.bbc.co.uk/music This website provides information, interviews, news, concert and programme listings about a wide range of musical styles, from classical to folk, jazz and pop.

Many composers and musicians have official websites. Type a name into a reliable search engine to find out more about them. Try **www.rvwsociety.com/** (for more about Vaughan Williams), **www.ericclapton.com/** or **www.courtneypine.co.uk/** to start you off.

Note to parents and teachers:
Every effort has been made by the Publishers to ensure that the websites in this book are suitable for children, that they are of the highest educational value, and that they contain no inappropriate or offensive material. However, because of the nature of the Internet, it is impossible to guarantee that the contents of these sites will not be altered. We strongly advise that Internet access is supervised by a responsible adult.

SOME PLACES TO VISIT

Dean's Yard, Westminster Abbey, London
You can visit the tombs of many great Britons, including Purcell, Handel and Vaughan Williams.

The Elgar Birthplace Museum, Lower Broadheath, Worcester
Visit Edward Elgar's birthplace, now a museum dedicated to him.

The Handel House Museum, 25 Brook Street, London WI
The London home of George Frideric Handel is now a museum.

Mendips, Liverpool and 20 Forthlin Road, Liverpool
Have a look around the childhood homes of two of the Beatles. Contact the National Trust for further information.

The Savoy Theatre, The Strand, London WC1
Book tickets to see one of Gilbert and Sullivan's operas.

Snape Maltings, Snape, Suffolk
Visit the concert hall where many of Benjamin Britten's works are still performed, or take a tour around his former home, The Red House, Aldeburgh, Suffolk.

Index

These are the lists of contents for each title in *Great Britons*:

LEADERS
Boudica • Alfred the Great • Richard I • Edward I • Robert Bruce
Owain Glyndwr • Henry V • Henry VIII • Elizabeth I
Oliver Cromwell • The Duke of Marlborough • Robert Walpole
Horatio Nelson • Queen Victoria • Benjamin Disraeli
William Gladstone • David Lloyd George • Winston Churchill
Clement Attlee • Margaret Thatcher

CAMPAIGNERS FOR CHANGE
John Wycliffe • John Lilburne • Thomas Paine • Mary Wollstonecraft
William Wilberforce • Elizabeth Fry • William Lovett
Edwin Chadwick • Lord Shaftesbury • Florence Nightingale
Josephine Butler • Annie Besant • James Keir Hardie • Emmeline Pankhurst
Eleanor Rathbone • Ellen Wilkinson • Lord David Pitt • Bruce Kent
Jonathon Porritt • Shami Chakrabati

NOVELISTS
Aphra Behn • Jonathan Swift • Henry Fielding • Jane Austen
Charles Dickens • The Brontë Sisters • George Eliot • Lewis Carroll
Thomas Hardy • Robert Louis Stevenson • Arthur Conan Doyle
Virginia Woolf • D H Lawrence • J R R Tolkien • George Orwell
Graham Greene • William Golding • Ian McEwan • J K Rowling
Caryl Phillips • Andrea Levy • Zadie Smith
Monica Ali • Salman Rushdie

ARTISTS
Nicholas Hilliard • James Thornhill • William Hogarth
Joshua Reynolds • George Stubbs • William Blake • J M W Turner
John Constable • David Wilkie • Dante Gabriel Rossetti
Walter Sickert • Gwen John • Wyndham Lewis • Vanessa Bell
Henry Moore • Barbara Hepworth • Francis Bacon • David Hockney
Anish Kapoor • Damien Hirst

ENGINEERS
Robert Hooke • Abraham Darby • James Watt • John MacAdam
Thomas Telford • George Cayley • George Stephenson • Robert Stephenson
Joseph Paxton • Isambard Kingdom Brunel • Henry Bessemer
Joseph Bazalgette • Joseph Whitworth • Charles Parsons • Henry Royce
Nigel Gresley • Lord Nuffield • Harry Ricardo • Frank Whittle • Norman Foster

SCIENTISTS
John Dee • Robert Boyle • Isaac Newton • Edmond Halley • William Herschel
Michael Faraday • Charles Babbage • Mary Anning • Charles Darwin
Lord Kelvin • James Clerk Maxwell • Ernest Rutherford • Joseph Rotblat
Dorothy Hodgkin • Alan Turing • Francis Crick • Stephen Hawking
John Sulston • Jocelyn Bell Burnell • Susan Greenfield

SPORTING HEROES
WG Grace • Arthur Wharton • Kitty Godfree • Roger Bannister
Stirling Moss • Jackie Stewart • Bobby Moore • George Best
Gareth Edwards • Barry Sheene • Ian Botham • Nick Faldo
Torville and Dean • Lennox Lewis • Daley Thompson • Steve Redgrave
Tanni Grey-Thompson • Kelly Holmes • David Beckham • Ellen McArthur

MUSICIANS
William Byrd • Henry Purcell • George Frideric Handel • Arthur Sullivan
Edward Elgar • Henry Wood • Ralph Vaughan Williams • Noel Coward
Michael Tippet • Benjamin Britten • Vera Lynn
John Dankworth and Cleo Laine • Jacqueline Du Pre
Eric Clapton • Andrew Lloyd Webber • Elvis Costello
Simon Rattle • The Beatles • Courtney Pine • Evelyn Glennie